Parables Lite

Twelve Parables of Jesus retold for two voices

Mike Stone

kevin
mayhew

First published in 2002 by
KEVIN MAYHEW LTD
Buxhall, Stowmarket, Suffolk, IP14 3BW
Email: info@kevinmayhewltd.com

9 8 7 6 5 4 3 2 1 0

ISBN 1 84003 914 0
Catalogue No 1500506

Front cover design by Angela Selfe
Edited by Elisabeth Bates
Typesetting by Louise Selfe

Printed and bound in Great Britain

Contents

For Monica – performer par excellence – and the people of St Michael's Church, Chichester, who encouraged these occasional alternatives to a sermon, laughed in the right places, and always saw the serious point of the story.

About the author

During a professional career in computer software, Mike Stone served his parish church as Reader and Non-stipendiary Priest. Retiring from these, he found activity working in a Christian bookshop, and has occasional opportunities of ministry in church and a pastoral concern among the elderly. He has nearly always seen the funny – even peculiar – side of church and Christian life.

Published works include *Introductions to the Lessons* (Columba, 2000), material widely used in churches which follow the Common Worship Lectionary.

Introduction

This book contains twelve Gospel parables, retold in a dialogue form, and one Gospel story written for four voices (though it can, if desired, be performed by two people).

Many of Jesus' parables seem to have been delivered to crowds. Some were shared only with the Twelve – we are told that some were explained to them – while most seem to have been left for the listeners to ponder. What we know of the creation of our four Gospels suggests that the evangelists were not often concerned with the original situations in which Jesus' brilliant and pungent anecdotes, epigrams and illustrations were told. They constructed their work from what had been remembered, and chose settings which suited that segment of their narrative.

I like to believe, from various hints in the text, that Jesus often played on people's sense of humour – isn't that, after all, a God-given grace unique to his human creatures? In retelling the stories, pious people have sometimes felt that laughter and religion do not go together. But for me, if something of that appeal to the funny bone can be restored, and the stories as we have them be filled out from what are clearly often no more than the bare bones of recollection, there may be renewed power in the message.

I take the liberty, then, of giving these thirteen pieces their own context – sometimes entirely modern, sometimes deliberately anachronistic. And I set out to provoke at least a smile, because alongside laughter, and indeed through it, may come a deeper sense of the serious point of Jesus' wonderful stories.

So, if you like your religion solemn and serious, BEWARE! God is laughing at you!

The sower and the seed

1	Once upon a seaside
2	Nice day!
1	Must've been
2	Crowds of people
1	Nice day out
2	Must've been.
1	Jesus got in a little boat
2	Nice day for it
1	Stood up
2	Very dangerous!
1	And told this story:
	PAUSE
2	Once upon a seedtime there was a farmer
1	Made a lot of money
2	Probably
1	From BSE compensation
2	European subsidies
1	Set-aside, stand-aside, five-a-side
2	Allegedly
1	One nice day
2	Went out with his sowing machine
1	A Singer?
2	No, farmer.
1	Anyway, this farmer

2   This *rich* farmer

1   Threw the seed just any old where

2   Could afford to;

1   In the field

2   Alongside the field

1   Among the thorns, the thistles and the thickets

2   Thometimeth

1   He even threw it over the useless rocky land

2   Which he'd sold off for housing

1   And over a footpath

2   A busy footpath

1   A right of way

2   Which was subject to Footpath Order No. 31 under Sub-section 5 of the Local Government Act of 1902 as amended by the Rural Conservation Resolution of the Countryside Commission.

1   So, when he came with his harrow

2   To plough the field

1   *After* scattering

2   The good seed on the land

1   – Well, that's how they did it –

2   He ploughed all through the field

1   But whistled at the thistles.

2   He left the stony bit for the bulldozers

1   Lots of ecology there

2   And lots of environment too;

1   But he ploughed up the footpath

2   The right of way

1   Which was subject to Footpath Order No. 31 under Sub-section . . .

2   That's the one.

1   So the Ramblers' Association objected

2   And the Pedestrians' Association complained

1   And the Football Association

2   Huh?

1   For the five-a-side

2   Oh

1   Complained to the civil authorities

2   Who stopped being civil and became quite rude;

1   Made the farmer restore the footpath

2   Flatten it all down again

1   So they could walk on it

2   Quite right too.

    PAUSE

1   Then, when the rains came down

2   And the crops came up

1   The corn on the footpath

2   Which was subject to Footpath Order No. 31 under . . .

1   That's the one

2   Which had been flattened for the walkers

1   And the hikers

2   And the bikers

1   The Ramblers

2   The Pedestrians

1   And the footballers

2   Going to play five-a-side

1   On the building site

2   Before the bulldozers moved in;

1   That seed on that footpath

2   Was eaten by the birds.

1   Meanwhile, the seed on the stony ground

2   Which was sold off for housing

1   Couldn't make roots and it died

2   No corn at all.

1   Meanwhile, the seed in the thistles

2   Never saw the light of day

1   Choked by the weeds

2   Not an ear of corn to be seen

1   Or heard

2   Too many weeds.

     PAUSE

1   Meanwhile, in the field

2   The corn grew as high

1   As an elephant-size packet of Kellogg's

2   Not ten times

1   Not fifty times

2   But a hundred times

1   More than he expected.

2   So the farmer got even richer! That's a good story. I like that.

     PAUSE

1   That's not the point,

2	Said Jesus.
1	The point is . . .
2	The point is?
1	God gets everywhere
2	Scattering seeds
1	Some for you
2	And some for me
1	Some for her
2	And some for him
1	And what do you do with it?
2	Said Jesus.
1	You can let the world walk all over you.
2	Some people are very shallow:
1	Some are pretty weedy:
2	But you can be like a very good field
1	A hundred acres
2	*Hectares!*
1	Same to you!
2	It's the Euroword.
1	*We* can be big fields
2	100-hectare fields producing hundredweights of harvest
1	Because Jesus said:
Both	The good soil is the person who hears the word of God and bears fruit.

King and country

1	Every year
2	Regularly
1	The summer goes south
2	For the winter.
1	In this story Jesus told
2	There was a royal family
1	Regularly went south
2	For the winter
1	Away from their kingdom
2	To their Winter Palace
1	For a rest from kinging
2	And queening
1	And signing things
2	And opening things
1	And day after day knighting people
2	And standing sideways
1	For postage stamp portraits
2	Giving weekly audiences
1	To the Chief Rabbi
2	The Speaker of the Sanhedrin
1	And the Chamberlain
2	Whose name was Neville.
	PAUSE

1   While the king was away

2   Neville

1   The Chamberlain

2   Was left in charge of the kingdom

1   With a small private army

2   To change the guard

1   The Mistress of the Wardrobe

2   To change the mothballs

1   All the Clerks to the Closet

2   Changing the loo-rolls

1   And all the Privy Council

2   Living lavishly.

1   Everything ran so smoothly

2   In the kingdom

1   People started saying

2   Who needs kings

1   And suchlike things?

2   The land is ours

1   With everything in it.

2   So, when the holiday postcard came:

1   'Having a right royal time

2   Boozing with the old folks

1   Saga louts

2   Love, Kingy and Queeny.

1   PS Don't do anything we wouldn't do.'

2   Neville

1   The Chamberlain

2   Replied by C-mail

1   (That's 'camel-mail')

2   'Anything you can do

1   I can do better.

2   I'm in charge now;

1   There'll be some changes here.

2   PS Don't bother to come back.'

     PAUSE

1   Well

2   The king wasn't bothered

1   Thought it was a joke

2   Sent a flunky

1   Just to see what was going on

2   And report back.

1   But the flunky never returned.

2   He was found dead

1   In the second-hand Body Shop

2   Neville had committed flunkicide

1   And life in the kingdom

2   Went from good to bad.

     PAUSE

1   Meanwhile

2   At the Winter Palace

1   When no news came

2   The king got worried

1   Was Neville doing things that ought not to have been done

2   And undoing things that ought to have been left done up?

1   Wondered what he should do.

2   Sent off another servant

1   Into his kingdom

2   A trained spy

1   Under cover

2   A plain brown cover

1   But he was uncovered

2   Not a good spy

1   A few double-O's short of seven

2   Dumped in the Dead Sea

1   Half-alive in a wooden overcoat

2   MI5?

1   No, MFI.

     PAUSE

2   And life in the kingdom

1   Went from bad to worse.

2   Meanwhile, back at the Winter Palace

1   The winter break

2   Had become a compound fracture.

1   The king was troubled

2   At the state of the kingdom

1   Which belonged to him

2   And everything in it.

1   He decided what to do.

2 'I'll now send my son

1 My own son, my own beloved son

2 Because everybody knows the principle

1 That one who is sent by a king

2 Is the same as the one who sends him

1 Because the royal presence

2 Cannot be divided.

1 My son can say

2 Whoever has seen me has seen my father

1 They will respect my son

2 Though he is only

1 The Prince of Dolphins'

2 (An ancient title

1 And the reason why the eldest sons

2 Of the kings of France

1 Were called The Dolphin)

2 But when the son

1 Came to the kingdom

2 Some of the people said

1 Look who it is!

2 See who it is!

1 The heir to the throne

2 The heir to the kingdom

1 Come on, let us kill him, and the inheritance will be ours

2 Others said

1 You can't kill him

2   Maybe he'll save us

1   From these bad times

2   Maybe the world would be a better place

1   If someone stopped Neville trying to make it a better place.

2   We do need a king

1   Someone to trust

2   Someone to follow

1   But . . .

2   The Chamberlain's private army arrested the king's son

1   And tried him for treason

2   And found him guilty

1   Took him outside the city

2   And hanged him.

PAUSE

1   What do you think of that?

2   Jesus asked those he was teaching.

1   They said: That's evil

2   Surely the King will reclaim his Kingdom

1   And give it to those who respected his Son

2   For his spirit lives on.

1   Even in his death there is new life

2   Wherever the Son is

1   There is the King

2   For ever and ever.

Thinking things through the looking-glass darkly

[A long way] After Lewis Carroll

1   Cathedral Green was bright and clean
      neat as a private place
2   No plastic bags, no doggie doos,
      of litter not a trace.
1   And this was odd, because it was
2   A very public space

1   The stonework stood majestically
      as good cathedrals do.
2   It loomed above the Green below
1   And rather spoiled the view
2   You could not see a soul, because
      the visitors were few.

1   The Canon and the Carpenter
2   Were walking close at hand.
1   They wept like anything to see
      deserted holy land.
2   'If we could put a tea shop here,'
      they said, 'It *would* be grand.'

1   'Dear layfolk, raise some funds with us,'
2   The Canon did implore.
1   'To build a tea shop on the Green
      with tourists round the door.
2   We'll need about a million pounds,
      perhaps a little more.'

1   'In Nazareth, where I come from,'
2   The Carpenter did say,
1   'We'd knock it up from four-by-two
      in less than half a day.
    But here we need good workmen who
      are worthy of their pay.'

2   'If seven men drew seven plans
       for forty days and nights,
     Do you suppose,' the Canon said,
       'we'd get the planning rights?'
1   'I hope so,' said the Carpenter;
       we'd call it "Sacred Bites".'

2   The eldest member shook his head.
       the cloisters were his home.
1   'Cathedrals stand for peace and God,
       not for the gastronome.
2   Shame on you that you think to add
       formica, glass and chrome.'

1   'The time has come,' the Canon said,
       'to talk of many things,
2   Of loos and lifts and ceiling-heights,
       and cantilevered springs,
1   And whether God will send the cash
       on flights of angel wings.'

2   But four young men had money skills
       in City suits and ties.
1   'Believe and trust in us,' they said,
       'have faith; you'll be surprised.'
2   And this was odd, because, you know,
       they hadn't been baptised.

1   The Carpenter from Nazareth
       rejoiced to hear them say,
2   'With diligence we'll think things through,
       and take your cares away.'
1   Good planning gets all good deeds done –
       makes good works seem like play.

2   'The time has come,' the Canon said,
       'To beg or steal or borrow.
1   We've made our plans, and that is wise,
       although there may be sorrow.
2   To make God laugh, just tell him what
       you plan to do tomorrow.'

1   *So, they had thought the funding through*

2   *However . . .*

1   'You are old, Canon Williams,' a young priest said,
        'and your hair has become very white,
     And yet you incessantly say, "Go ahead".
        How can you be sure you are right?'

2   'In my youth,' Canon Williams explained to the lad,
        'I was sure that I always knew best.
     But now I have found that the whole world is mad,
        so I simply ignore all the rest.'

1   'You are old,' said the youth, 'and I want to be fair,
        but you may not have noticed the law.
     You will need six permissions to build anywhere;
        the Council will hate what you draw.'

2   'In my youth,' said the sage, 'I saw Aldermen flower,
        and democracy wore a clean coat.
     Now I've learnt where to lean on the levers of power.
        They'll say "Yes" without even a vote.'

1   'You are old,' said the priest, 'and you may have a fight.
        Conservation will win, I believe.
     Our Green, as you know, is a Heritage Site,
        with its tree and the statue of Eve.'

2   'You are young,' said the Canon, 'you've not understood
        that the tree in the midst of the garden
     Was put there to help us tell evil from good.
        I'll just fell it and then ask for pardon.'

1   'You are old,' said the youth, 'one would hardly suppose
        that your eye was as steady as ever.
     Yet you see how to deal with all of your foes.
        what makes you so awfully clever?'

2   'I've answered three questions; we'll have no more ado,'
        said the Canon. 'Don't give yourself airs.
     There are battles to win, and I've thought them all through.
        Now get out and get on with your prayers.'

1   *So, six months later . . .*

2   The Canon and the Carpenter
        took tea at half-past four
1   And thick and fast the thirsty came
        and more, and more, and more –
    All crowding in the tea-shop now
        and queuing at the door.

2   The Carpenter from Nazareth
1   (Whose name you will have guessed)
2   Said, 'Bring some bread and bring some wine,
        let's celebrate with zest.
    The table's laid, the hungry fed,
        our plans have met the test.

1   'If you desire to build a tower,
        sit down and count the cost.
2   And if you have a war to win
        think how it might be lost.
1   So if you plan to follow me
        remember I was crossed.'

2   They celebrated with a feast
        a teapot like a chalice.
1   The Bishop came in radiant pink –
        the best dress in the Palace –
2   And this was not thought odd, because
        the Bishop's name was – Alice.

A fair day's work

1   Once there was a vineyard

2   Lots of vineyards in the Bible

1   Good land for wine

2   Palestine

1   Lots of rain, lots of shine

2   In *this* vineyard

1   At harvest-time

2   Lots of grape-pickers needed

1   So Philip

2   Who owned this vineyard

1   Went to the Job Centre

2   The Labour Exchange

1   New Labour, New Start

2   New name, same paperwork

1   Philip put up a notice

2   'Men wanted'

1   Sexist!

2   Oh all right. Strong, burly, muscular people wanted

1   That's better

2   Wanted tomorrow

1   One day only

2   Harvesting grapes

1   Pick your own booze

2	Full day's work guaranteed
1	Full day's pay promised
	PAUSE
2	And guess what?
1	Six o'clock next morning
2	Nobody turned up
1	Typical idle layabouts
2	Stop their benefits!
1	Well, it was a cold morning
2	Cold as a dachshund's nose
1	But when the sun came up
2	Crowds turned up
1	Men and women
2	Standing bumper to bumper
1	For their scissors and baskets
2	Expecting cash in hand
1	At the end of the day.
	PAUSE
2	Come lunchtime
1	Baguettes and *grappa al fresco*
2	Very exotic foreign
1	Three angry young men turned up
2	What were they angry about?
1	Life, I think
2	They disapproved of it
1	It's an occupational hazard

2	Of those with no occupation
1	So Philip gave them a job
2	For the rest of the day.
	PAUSE
1	At half-past three
2	Time for tea
1	Everyone could see
2	More help was needed
1	So Philip jumped in his van
2	Down to the Job Centre
1	To see if the labour pool
2	Had anyone left in the shallow end
1	Left to their own vices.
2	He picked up a few waifs and strays
1	No one else had wanted
2	The kind of people
1	Who seem to be caused by accident
2	He took them to the vineyard
1	For a short evening's shift
2	In dayglo overalls.
1	Odd how God
2	Finds work to do
1	For those
2	The world thinks useless.
1	So the day wore on
2	And the fun wore off

1	And they were all worn out
2	Some more than most
1	Come sunset
2	The grapes were all cut
1	Ready for pressing
2	And Philip was impressed
1	So it was pay-out time
2	And guess what?
1	The last came first
2	Naturally
1	Expecting just a couple of quid
2	Naturally
1	For a couple of hours' work
2	Of course
1	Got a full day's pay
2	Amazing
1	So, they said:
2	Thanks very much, squire
1	Very kind of you, squire
2	Very generous, Your Graciousness
1	Yes, it was
2	And next the three angry young men
1	Who had come at noon
2	Also got a full day's pay
1	Not hungry or angry now
2	Very generous and gracious

1   You're a man from the top drawer

2   That never gets stuck.

1   So, those who worked two hours

2   Got a day's pay

1   And those who did a half-day

2   Got a day's pay

1   What about those who worked all day?

2   *They* got a day's pay

1   That's not fair

2   They said

1   We may be well fed

2   But we're well fed-up

1   We've been busy as beetles

2   What about the hard day's right?

1   We've been here

2   They said

1   Since time immoral

2   We should get more

1   They said

2   And you might think so

1   But Philip said

2   Jesus said

1   You agreed what was fair

2   And I want to be generous and gracious

1   To other people

2   Because their needs are the same as yours

1   And in my vineyard

2   Which is the kingdom of heaven

1   There should be no complaints

2   Because I am generous to everyone

1   Because I know their needs

2   And I love to give

1   Not what you deserve or desire

2   But what you most need

1   Said Jesus

2   And every now and then

1   When you say

2   Kingdom come

1   Remember it is *my* kingdom

2   Where there are no firsts nor lasts

1   But everyone has everything

2   For ever.

Be at the church on time

1	In a little village
2	Deep in Palestine
1	Jesus was walking along
2	Quietly
1	With his 12 Decibels
2	And he told them this story:
	PAUSE
1	There was once a village wedding
2	Oi vay! and Hallelujah!
1	Lovely bride
2	They always are
1	Handsome groom
2	That's unusual
1	Everything prepared
2	According to the usual arrangements
1	An arranged marriage
2	By the matchmaker
1	Which was handy
2	Matches were needed
1	To light the torches
2	The oil-lamp torches
1	According to the usual arrangements
2	Because wedding days began at dusk

1 So come the sunset

2 All the women crowded in

1 To the bride's house

2 To wait for the groom to arrive

1 With all the other men

2 Into the bride's home

1 And have the wedding there

2 As was usual.

PAUSE

1 Everything in faultless taste

2 No tasteless faults

1 Everything well prepared

2 Nothing left to chance

1 Hairdresser had been

2 Bride's hair all set

1 To go off in an hour

2 Dad had a clip round the ear

1 And then went out

2 As usual

1 Mum cooking and cooking

2 Cordon Blue in the face

1 All the ten bridesmaids

2 Virgins

1 Possibly

2 Not virgins?

1 Symbolically, but not technically

2	On hire from Richard Branson
1	According to the usual arrangements
2	They had to hold the torches –
1	The oil-lamps.
	PAUSE
2	As the evening wore on
1	And turned into night
2	The bride waited
1	For her knight in shining 'jamas
2	All prepared
1	Nothing left to chance
2	Waiting for him to come
1	Watching and waiting
2	He was nowhere to be seen
1	Not strictly true
2	He *could* be seen
1	In a different place
2	Out with the boys
1	Enjoying his camel-night out
2	(No stags in Palestine)
1	Time ticked on
2	No groom
1	Still room for the groom
2	The virgins'
1	Bridesmaids'
2	Arms got tired

1 Put down their torches

2 Put them out

1 Sat down

2 Sat around

1 Like filleted earwigs

2 In the dark

1 Waiting.

PAUSE

2 Midnight struck

1 There was a shouting

2 A hollering

1 Yoo-hoo!

2 Coo-ee!

1 He's coming!

2 Coo-err!

1 Up with the torches

2 Out with the matches

1 Light up the lamps

2 Oh dear

1 Oh dearie me

2 Half the ten bridesmaids

1 Five of the virgins

2 Sadly discovered they'd run out of oil

1 Hadn't been prepared

2 For the long wait

1 Not enough oil

2   To see them through the night

1   Oh foolish virgins!

2   Asked the other five

1   Give us a lend

2   Lend us some oil

1   But they couldn't

2   Although they were wise

1   And well-prepared

2   Not enough to spare

1   To light the foolish ones' as well

2   So it was on with the coats

1   Quick! He's coming!

2   On with the shoes

1   He's coming!

2   Run down to One-Stop

1   Open all hours

2   But it wasn't

1   So round to the all-night garage

2   For a quick pint of lamp-oil

1   Back to the house

2   Found the door shut

1   Groom gone in

2   Wedding under way

1   As arranged by the matchmaker

2   Who refused to let them in

1   As was usual

2   Because, if you weren't there

1   When the bridegroom arrived

2   You couldn't be part of the party

1   If you weren't there

2   Ready and waiting

1   Watching for him to come.

PAUSE

2   That's the way it was

1   Said Jesus

2   And he says to us

1   Keep watching for me

2   I am coming

1   Keep waiting for me

2   I am coming

1   Be prepared

2   Stay awake

1   Stay alert

2   When he comes

1   You'll want to join the party

2   Not be left out

1   From the great wedding banquet

2   The feast in his kingdom

1   He's coming

2   He's coming

1   Maranatha

2   Come, Lord Jesus.

The JP

1   Hello

2   Hello

1   Peace be with you

2   And justice with you.

1   In the *Bumper Book of Best Bible Bits*

2   Usually called Gospels

1   There is this story.

    PAUSE

2   Jesus said:

1   Once there was a widow woman

2   Not a very merry widow

1   Called Yolande* Bluekettle

2   Funny name

1   Better than her married name

2   Which was Yolande

1   Hoy

2   Not very merry

1   She was not a happy soul

2   Said Jesus

1   A litigious recidivist, said Jesus.

2   Did he?

1   In Aramaic, of course

* Note: 3 syllables YO-LAND-ER

2	Good language. What did he mean?
1	She was always going to law
2	In and out of the courts
1	Like a ball-boy at Wimbledon
2	Anything she didn't like
1	She'd find a law against it
2	And report it
1	To the police
2	To Trading Standards
1	The council
2	Ofgas, Ofwat
1	Offside, off course
2	And the local magistrates.
1	If people break the law
2	She thought
1	They ought to be stopped
2	She said.
1	Bit of a busy-body, then
2	Well-known in eccentric circles
1	For her persistence.
2	There ought to be a law
1	Against people like that.
	PAUSE
2	The annoying thing was
1	She was usually right
2	So she got plenty of justice

1   But no one else got any peace

2   Especially Zephaniah, Obediah and Habakkuk

1   Solicitors to God

2   And especially Sir William Smith, DD, PG

1   Bar mitzvah and Bar

2   JP

1   J for Justice

2   P for Peace

1   Who sat on the bench

2   Though he preferred an armchair

1   Whose job it was to listen to complaints

2   To hear people swear

1   To make court orders

2   To watch over local justice

1   To bind people over

2   To keep the peace

1   But not a good JP

2   Said Jesus

1   Not a good listener

2   Who is?

1   Didn't listen to God

2   Who does?

1   Nor to public opinion

2   So single-minded

1   He wouldn't have double-glazing

2   And this awful lawful widow

1 Who kept pestering for justice

2 Was such a nuisance

1 He got no peace.

2 Sometimes he wouldn't answer the door

1 Or the answering machine

2 Or the e-mails

1 And he even set up a website

2 WWW dot

1 Weird Widow Woman dot asterisk dot exclamation mark dot bleep dot dot dot dot

2 He sometimes thought

1 In strong Anglo-sexist language

2 That loud asterisk bleep women ought not to be allowed.

1 But she kept knocking

2 And writing

1 And phoning,

2 And e-mailing

1 So he could get no peace

2 Until he had given her justice.

PAUSE

1 And the lesson for us

2 Said Jesus

1 Is *not* that God doesn't listen

2 Because he always listens

1 And *not* that God doesn't answer

2 Because he always answers.

1 What we must do

2	Said Jesus

1	Is to persist in praying

2	To keep praying for justice

1	And praying for peace

2	It's good to keep asking

1	Especially in prayer

2	God loves to hear our prayer

1	Doesn't he just!

2	So keep asking God, JP

1	For all that you desire

2	That's what he's there for

1	So persist in prayer

2	Make God happy today!

1	Keep on praying

2	Said Jesus

1	And go in peace.

A family business

1	There was a family business
2	Johnson
1	And Son
2	And Son
1	A travel business
2	Whose slogan was
1	'We get you there –
2	Make your own way back.'
1	Bill and Ben
2	The two Johnson sons
1	Were business men
2	About their father's business
1	Bill was older
2	Ben was younger
1	Bill – the son and heir –
2	Arranged other people's sun and air
1	Bill never went on holiday
2	Never took a day off
1	Worked very hard
2	Nose to the grindstone, fingers to the bone, ear to the ground, one foot on the ladder, and back to the wall
1	Sounds precarious.
	PAUSE
2	Unlike Bill, the son and heir

1	Ben got in everyone's hair
2	Ben
1	The younger son
2	Was idle
1	Took all the free trips
2	In all the brochures
1	Took lots of days off
2	For friends' grandmothers' weddings
1	Getting the car serviced
2	At a drive-in church
1	Visiting all his girlfriends
2	The well-known beauty spots
1	It couldn't go on
2	It didn't
1	Ben asked Dad Johnson
2	For a Sabbatical
1	Every Saturday off
2	His father said
1	Tell you what I'll do:
2	Take your share of the business
1	As cash in lieu
2	Decide where you want to go
1	And we'll get you there – find your own way back
2	So Ben took the money and flew off to Southern Ireland
1	By air to Eire
2	Found a nice little town as seen on TV

· 1   Called Bally-kick-devil

2   He joined in all the high life with the publicans

1   And the low life with the sinners

2   Spend, spend, spend

1   All that cash in lieu

2   Was money down the drain

      PAUSE

1   Down to the last few Irish punts

2   Oh dear

1   No more square meals

2   One round meal a day

1   At McDonald's

2   Oh dear!

1   Saved money by wearing only one sock at a time

2   Had to get a job

1   Tried an undertaker

2   Lasted two weeks as a trainee corpse

1   Tried a security firm

2   Sacked for lying about his height

1   Tried McDonald's

2   Oh dear!

1   Paddy McDonald's *Farm*

2   Here a cluck, there a moo

1   Everywhere an Irish oink-oink

2   Early morning alarm cocks going off

1   Too much noise and smell

2	Too much Irish stew
1	Ben ended up on the streets
2	Street cleaning
1	Really in the gutter
2	And suddenly thought
1	Hang on!
2	He thought
1	Hang about a bit!
2	He said
1	This is ridiculous
2	I could shift rubbish at home
1	Cleaning Dad's travel shop
2	If I go home and say sorry
1	Forgive me, Dad; I'm not worth treating as a son
2	Take me on as an office cleaner
1	He might forgive me and take me in.
2	So he hitched
1	And he hiked
2	Made his own way back
1	And got home, where the family business
2	Was still Johnson
1	And Son
2	And Son
1	And Ben said
2	Forgive me, Dad; I'm not worth treating as a son
1	Take me on as an office cleaner.

PAUSE

2   What he didn't know

1   Could never have guessed

2   Dad Johnson had been looking for him every day

1   Watching and waiting while he was still far off

2   Welcomed him now with open arms

1   Opened all the doors

2   Opened all the windows

1   Shouted down the street

2   Ben's come back!

1   Ben's come home!

2   Let's have a party

1   Break out the best bubbly Bollinger

2   Get him a new shirt someone

1   Clean the Irish bog off his boots

2   The shamrock off his shoulders

1   And for goodness sake get him a decent haircut.

2   Meanwhile

1   A bare ten minutes away

2   The fully clothed Bill

1   Remember him?

2   The elder son and heir

1   Had been at work

2   Making his own way back

1   As he did every day

2   Was shocked

1   Shaken and stirred

2   To find a party going on

1   Ben's come back!

2   Hmph!

1   Back from Ireland

2   Hmph!

1   Repented his Eire

2   So what?

1   Join in the party!

2   Shan't

1   He sulked all the way to his bedroom

2   'What's the good of me working my fingers to the bone,
        nose to the grindstone all year long,
        going to church every Sunday, saying my prayers,
        if you're going to be prodigal with your love and forgiveness
        to this son of yours who doesn't deserve it?
        And by the way, when did I last get a free haircut?'

1   Because Bill didn't know

2   Though he should have guessed

1   That his father loved him just as much as Ben

2   It's just that

1   There's more joy over a son who makes his own way back

2   Than a faithful son who never goes away

1   And isn't it grand

2   To have a father whose prodigality of love never runs out?

1   Prodigally PRODIGALIDOCIOUS!

Pardon me for praying

1   Miss Emily Salter

2   Pillar of the community

1   And lovely with it

2   Was always in church

1   Every Sunday

2   Naturally

1   Morning and evening

2   Of course

1   Also on Mondays

2   Unusual

1   And Tuesdays

2   Quite unusual

1   And every other day too

2   Very unusual

PAUSE

1   Unfortunately

2   Miss Emily Salter

1   Who was lovely with it

2   Treated the church like home

1   Her own home

2   And took on all the housework

1   Honorary vestry virginning

2   Every pew polished

1   Every statue washed behind the ears

2   Sundries done and dusted

1   No linen unpurified

2   No wicks untrimmed

1   No altar unaltered

2   No holes in holy vestments

1   No flowers

2   Except by arrangement

1   But she was lovely with it

2   And no prayer was left unprayed

1   Because Emily did love God

2   Unusual

1   She loved the church

2   Quite unusual

1   Loved herself

2   Naturally

1   But unfortunately

2   She forgot to love her neighbour as herself

        PAUSE

1   So one Friday morning

2   She prayed

1   As usual

2   Thank you, God

1   That's good

2   Thank you, God, for being good to me

1   For leading me to do the right things and fulfil all my duties

2   The cleaning duties

1   The flower duties

2   The verging duties

1   And telling the vicar what his vital religious support role is.

2   Thank you, Lord, that when I did the Alpha course

1   I got Beta plus

2   Thank you, Lord, that I'm not like other people

1   In particular

2   Very particularly not like

1   That Malcolm

2   Pillock of the community

1   Behind that pillar

2   Trying to hide

1   Kneeling down

2   Praying

1   Praying!

2   In *my* church!

PAUSE

1   Now Malcolm

2   Unfortunately

1   Was no better than he should be

2   And often a great deal worse

1   Been a bad lad

2   Tell us about it!

1   Wasted his substance

2   On illegal substances

1   Petty criminal

2	Burgling houses
1	Lifting shops
2	Fond of the horses
1	No stable relationships
2	In hot water
1	So many times
2	He looked like a teabag
1	Unfortunately
2	Very bad reputation
1	Taken into custody
2	For every trifle
1	Did time
2	Several times
1	A life punctuated by short sentences
2	Came to a full stop
1	When he discovered
2	On an Alpha course
1	Naturally
2	That he could be saved from his sins
1	Malcolm saw the light
2	At one o'clock in the morning
1	Found the Good News in the Gospel
2	Matthew, Mark, Luke and John
1	Went through life with their heads screwed on
2	He'd never been an atheist
1	Just God's loyal opposition

2   So this Friday

1   In church

2   Malcolm prayed

1   I'm so sorry,

2   I'm very, very sorry

    PAUSE

1   Huh!

2   Thought Miss Emily

1   That's all very well

2   Never mind being sorry

1   Mend your ways

2   Be like other people

1   Like me

    PAUSE

2   And Jesus said

1   That Malcolm

2   The sinner

1   A very sorry sinner

2   Went home

1   More right with God

2   Than lovely Emily Salter

1   Who thought she was right

2   But she was wrong

1   While Malcolm

2   Said Jesus

1   Knew he was wrong

2   So he was right.

1   That can't be right

2   Unfortunately

1   Said Jesus

2   Knowing you are wrong is right

1   How very unusual

2   He often is.

The pearl and the treasure

(Voice 1 must be male, voice 2 female)

1   Good morning from her

2   And good morning from him

1   I'm him

2   I'm her

1   Man

2   And wife

1   Tall and handsome

2   Petite and elegant

1   2 metres 3 in his designer boots

2   5 foot 4 in Centigrade

1   He spends his day

2   She spends her day

1   In the heart of the City

2   In the depths of the country

1   Near to the Mansion House

2   Near fields and farms

1   Near to the Temple

2   Near the Parish Church

1   Busy husband

2   Idle wife

1   He deals in high finance

2   She's a financial disaster zone

1   Merchant banking

2	Flower arranging
1	Insider trading
2	No outside interests
1	Stocks and shares
2	Hoover the stairs
1	Sat with the money-changers
2	Sat with gossip exchangers
1	Travelled the world's stock markets
2	Went to the farmer's market
1	Quick turnover
2	Apple turnover
1	Not at all happy
2	Not at all satisfied
1	Something missing in life
2	Something important missing
1	Like a peep-toe wellington boot
2	Like a cling-film frying pan
1	You get the picture
Both	We get the picture.
	PAUSE
1	This is his story:
2	On a business trip
1	Coming back from Tokyo
2	Got sick at the airport
1	Terminal illness
2	From eating too much salmon

1	With salmonella
2	Sushi and chips
1	Saki and chopsticks
2	And lots of oysters
1	With real pearls
2	Was very, very ill
1	Heart-stoppingly ill
2	A near-death experience
1	Had a vision
2	Of the Pearly Gates
1	Saw St Peter
2	The Pearly- Gate keeper
1	Lots of pearly kings and queens
2	Pearly saints and saintesses
1	Even saw St Homobonus
2	The patron saint of businessmen
1	(That's true!)
2	But his vision faded
1	Came back to life
2	Wondering what life was all about
1	And what was worthwhile
2	Whether there was one thing
1	Worth more than anything.
2	Then he saw it
1	A real pearl
2	Not a Pearly Gate

1	A true pearl
2	Nearly priceless
1	How much?
2	Somewhere north of a million quid
1	So he sold all his shares
2	Divested his investments
1	Collected his collateral
2	Ditched his dollars
1	And used up his Euros
2	To buy the one thing worth sacrificing everything for

PAUSE

1	It's his poor wife I feel sorry for
2	No need to be
1	This is her story:
2	One fine day
1	Walking in the fields
2	With a metal detector
1	(As you do)
2	She got an attack of the bleeps
1	A detectoring bleep
2	The detector detecting
1	Buried treasure
2	It wasn't her field
1	Couldn't dig for treasure
2	So she kept very quiet
1	Raided her piggy-bank

2   Had a sale of old boots

1   Pawned the chess set

2   De-mutualised her Building Society savings

1   Hatched her nest-egg

2   And got just enough money

1   To buy the field

2   With its treasure

1   Got digging

2   Hot diggety!

1   Very secretly

2   And dug up a vast treasure

1   More than she could desire or deserve

2   What sort of treasure?

1   Ancient archaeological artefacts

2   Nearly priceless

1   Somewhere south of a million quid

2   She gave everything she had

1   To get one thing worth sacrificing everything for

PAUSE

Both   So:

1   He had sacrificed everything for a pearl

2   She had sacrificed everything for buried treasure

1   And he rejoiced

2   And she rejoiced

1   What he had

2   What she had

1   Was worth more than everything else you could think of

2   And Jesus says

1   When you discover something

2   Better than anything else

1   Be prepared to sacrifice everything

2   For the pearl

1   For the treasure

2   And my kingdom is the best thing

1   In this world and the next

2   It's worth giving everything it takes

1   To take hold of the kingdom

2   This kingdom is the one thing

Both   Worth sacrificing everything for.

Pennies in heaven

1   There once was a man

2   Said Jesus

1   As he often did

2   And this man

1   Didn't get where he was today

2   By giving his money away

1   And where he was today

2   Was very comfortably rich, thank you.

1   So rich

2   The banks came to him for money

1   He was a specialist collector

2   Specialising in money

1   Not just a coin-collector

2   Not a *nu*mismatist

1   But an old miser

2   With a capital MY

1   Was very good at business

2   His only good deeds

1   Were property deeds

2   Playing Monopoly for real

1   Made a fortune

2   A property magnate

1   Attracting iron buildings

2   Arranged loans

1   At highly interesting rates

2   Sat on lots of boards

1   And comfortable chairs

2   Ran a commercial college

1   Pay As You Learn

2   Very good head for money

1   With a slot across the top.

2   Collected money

1   Saved it

2   Stored it

1   Hoarded it

2   Counted it

1   Never heard the proverb

2   Early to bed

1   Early to rise

2   Makes a man

1   Wealthy

2   Selfish

1   And dead

2   Couldn't stop collecting money

1   Something in his genes

2   The back pocket of his genes

         PAUSE

1   Until one day he decided

2   Too much was enough

1   Time to take it easy

2   Could eat, drink and enjoy

1   Live it up a little at night

2   Stay in bed late

1   Never see dawn from the front

2   Do a little gentle spending

1   Of all he had collected

2   All that cash

1   Used notes tied up in bundles

2   All over the house

1   Shelves full of shekels

2   Drawers full of drachmae

1   Demijohns of denarii

2   Needed more space

1   For all that cash

2   So he bought a farm

1   A dairy farm

2   Flowing with milk and money

1   Built lots of big barns

2   To store his money mountain

1   So big

2   They had to be seen to be boggled at.

1   Moved in

2   And settled down to the quiet life

1   Counting his pennies

2   Until God said

1   Oi! you daft hap'orth

2   I've been watching your life

1   All your days are counted

2   And your number's up – tonight.

1   He couldn't believe it

2   Took no notice

1   Stuck his head in the sand

2   Which left other parts exposed

1   Didn't feel at death's door

2   Not even walking up the drive

1   But next morning

2   He woke up dead.

1   And if you're dead

2   There's nothing to do

1   But lie back and enjoy it.

2   The doctor said

1   It was a rush of blood to the wallet

2   Though of course the rich man didn't hear that

1   Because death may be only a sleep

2   But it's a lot harder to get up in the morning

1   And he woke to life after death

2   Without his cash collection

1   No need for pennies in heaven

2   His collection

1   Was no use to him now

2   Can't take it with you.

1   And God said

2   Sorry, you can't eat and drink and enjoy your collection.

1   You collected money

2   But I collect people

1   And I enjoy my collecting.

2   Death is not the end

1   God said.

2   You have been foolish

1   But not bad

2   And fools are readily forgiven

1   When they realise their folly

2   And I turn no one away.

1   So God said

2   You've left your house

1   And your farm

2   Come into the mansion I have prepared for you

1   And make new friends.

PAUSE

2   But God says to us

1   You should live life my way.

2   Instead of spending your life

1   Making money for yourself

2   You should spend your money

1   Making life for others

2   Money should be a means to an end

1   Not the end of your means

2   Don't store your treasure in barns

1   Or cupboards

2   Or sideboards

1   Without ever thinking

2   To store up some riches in heaven

Both   Collecting money is bad!

The house builders

1	Hello
2	Good morning
1	Nice day
2	For a holiday
1	On the Mediterranean
2	Where there's a town called Joppa
1	Joppa-sur-Mer
2	Like Bognor by the Sea
1	Joppa *Regis*
2	Because King David once said
1	'Don't like Joppa,'
2	When he went through in nine-fifty-six
1	Though the record has since been broken
2	A dull place, Joppa
1	Where the tide went out one day
2	And didn't bother to come back
1	But the population was growing
2	People wanted seaside homes
1	Wanted to move to the coast
2	To escape the Inland Revenue
1	So in Joppa by the Sea
2	On a steep hill
1	Straight up from the beach
2	Signboards went up

1   Plots for sale

2   Self-build houses

1   Build what you like

2   Where you like

1   Anywhere on the hillside

2   Two up

1   Two down

2   And two further down

1   For the foundations

2   Two garages

1   Two incomes

2   And one-point-nought children.

PAUSE

1   Now there were two men

2   Said Jesus

1   He often did

2   Two men

1   Willy and Wally

2   Did he say that?

1   No, but names are useful

2   Willy and Wally

1   Had a lot in common

2   Two wives

1   Each?

2   No, monogamy

1   That's a good wood!

2 Glorious Goodwood!

1 Both self-made men

2 (To a design by God)

1 Both liked DIY

2 Both fancied self-build homes

1 But Willy was smarter

2 His body language

1 Was in italics

2 While Wally

1 Was a bit hard of thinking

2 Both liked music

1 Willy liked The Three Tenors

2 Josè, Placido and Luciano

1 But Wally liked The Three Fivers

2 Josè Sprinkler, Flaccid Flamingo and Lucy Anne Rotweiler

1 Both men were made in the image of God

2 But some are more than others

1 So while Willy won Thinker of the Year award

2 By picking a plot at the *top* of the hill

1 Where he could see for miles

2 One mile from the sea

1 Wally chose one at the bottom

2 Wally liked being on the shore

1 Quite sure

2 That all that sand

1 Just needed a ton of cement

2   To turn it into respectable pavement

PAUSE

1   So the self-build houses began

2   Willy's house at the top

1   Two up

2   Two down

1   And two further down

2   For the foundations

1   All main services

2   Gas, Electricity, Water

1   Phone and Fax and Cable TV

2   Wall-to-wall floor

1   And inside lounge

2   Willy moved in

1   With Milly and Tilly

2   His wife and his daughter

1   Settled down on the hilltop

2   Liked the views

1   Clean air

2   And solid foundations

1   And lived happily ever after.

2   But Wally

1   Whose family tree

2   Produced only nuts

1   Built near the beach

2   And his self-build Manual

1   Had the last pages missing

2   An appendectomy

1   So when he built his house

2   Two up

1   And two down

2   He forgot the two further down

1   For the foundations

2   And when Wally moved in

1   With Mollie and Polly

2   His wife and his daughter

1   He got his gas from the Electricity Board

2   Electricity from the Water Board

1   And water through the floorboards

2   The summer was fine

1   With lovely sea views

2   And walks along the front

1   One minute from the beach

2   But winter came

1   And the tide got higher

2   And the rain came down

1   And the wind got up

2   And the storms swelled the rivers

1   Water, water, everywhere

2   And Wally's foundations

1   (Which he'd forgotten to build)

2   Were washed away

1   Silly Wally

2   If he had a star sign

1   It was Soggy-trousers.

PAUSE

2   Wally phoned Floodline

1   Who said, 'You're flooded!'

2   He called the Environment Agency

1   Whose computer said, 'All of our agents are busy right now

2   If you would like to leave a message

1   Please remember you can press 76213998312470'

2   Wally said

1   'Help!'

2   But his house fell down

1   Because it had no foundation

PAUSE

2   Which just goes to show

1   Said Jesus

2   That you can't build your life

1   On a sea view

2   One minute from the beach

1   But no foundations

2   Because when bad times come

1   Where will you find strength?

2   And the foundation Jesus wants for us

1   Is to hear his teaching

2   And to be rooted and grounded in it

1   Built on the rock of faith.

Rich man, poor man

1   Once there was a rich man

2   Daidle deedle, daidle, digguh, digguh, deedle, daidle, dum*

1   Lived in style

2   Very high style

1   Highly des. res.

2   10 bed, 2 recep.

1   6 bed en-suite

2   And 4 not so sweet

1   High wall all round

2   Security TV cameras all round

1   Money passed through his hands

2   Without touching the sides

1   Made a million a day

2   Never gave any away

1   Especially to beggars

2   Or the homeless

1   Like Lazarus

2   Who lived in a cardboard box

1   Outside the rich man's back gate

2   Where there was a notice

* 'If I Were A Rich Man' from *Fiddler on the Roof*

Dai - dle,   dee - dle,   dai - dle,   dig - guh,   dig - guh,   dee - dle,   dai - dle,   dum.

1   'No hawkers, no circulars, no squatters'.

2   But Lazarus had nothing to hawk

1   And he wasn't circular

2   And he didn't squat

1   So he sat there

2   Begging

1   Hoping for scraps from the kitchen

2   Poor Lazarus just sat all day

1   With only his two dogs for company

2   And the television

1   . . . security camera . . .

2   Keeping watch on him day and night

1   And while the rich man ate like a bird

2   Seven times his body weight every day

1   Lazarus and his dogs had very little

2   And some days nothing at all.

     PAUSE

1   Now this rich man

2   Call him 'Dives'

1   Why?

2   It's Greek for a rich man

1   So, Dives

2   Safe in his mansion

1   Never thinking to feed Lazarus

2   Got old and died

1   Couldn't take it with him

2   Never believed the Bible

1   Or the Rabbis

2   So was very surprised

1   To find himself in hell

2   Which he didn't believe in

1   With a superb view of heaven

2   Which he didn't believe in either

1   Because he thought theology

2   Was only useful

1   For teaching other people theology

2   And for the first time in his life

1   Someone had told him where to go.

     PAUSE

2   And then poor Lazarus died

1   What about his dogs?

2   They went to Mount Goddy*

1   The Holy House for Homeless Hounds

2   As for Lazarus

1   He found himself in heaven

2   With a superb view of Abraham, Isaac and Co.

1   Lucky beggar

2   Not to mention David and Solomon and prophets galore

1   For theirs is the kingdom of heaven

2   Who said that?

1   Can't quite remember.

* A pun on the name of our RSPCA Sanctuary. Adapt to local circumstances

2 And next life around, after this life

1 It's the poor what gets the pleasure

2 And the rich what gets the shame

1 Is that justice?

2 Not necessarily, but it's in the story.

  PAUSE

1 Well, down in the fiery place

2 That he didn't believe in

1 Dives was steaming

2 Tried to sit

1 For a bit

2 Far too hot

1 Even to squat

2 No joke

1 All that smoke

2 Like eating light bulbs

1 And he noticed Lazarus

2 About time too!

1 With Abraham

2 In heaven

1 Dives begged for a drink

2 Just water

1 To cool his tongue

2 Perrier, Highland Spring or Portsmouth* tap

1 It's what they put in it, innit?

* Substitiute the name of your town

2   But Abraham said

1   No way

2   Because there is no way

1   From heaven to hell and back again

2   No way?

1   No way

2   People ought to know about that

1   They could

2   If they read their Bible

1   People should

2   And they listened to the Rabbis

1   People should

2   And listened to the priests and prophets

1   Then they'd know

2   But they don't believe in heaven or hell.

1   You'd think God would make it clear

2   Send someone from heaven

1   Or hell . . .!

2   To make sure we know about it

1   Someone like Lazarus

2   Or Jesus

1   So everyone would know

2   But they don't listen

1   Not even to one raised from the dead

2   If that ever happened

1   If someone came back from the dead

2	Like Jesus
1	You'd think people would listen
2	But they don't
1	Like the poet said:
2	'Man will not change for one voice crying truth'*
1	Still, it makes you think
2	If you have ears to hear, then hear
1	Now who was it said that?
2	Can't quite remember.

* Masefield, *The Coming of Christ*

The well-woman

A piece for four voices (Note: This piece can be performed by two voices only, but it is best if voice 3 is male, and voice 4 female.)

1   Fancy a story?

2   Well, here's a good one.

1   One day, Jesus and his friends were going home from Jerusalem

2   Been on holiday?

1   No, holy day

2   Same thing really

1   Could be, even in Jerusalem.

2   So, going back to Galilee

1   Sixty-mile journey

2   Took a few days

1   Used the short cut

2   Through Samaria

1   Where Jews weren't popular

2   Like Protestants and Catholics

1   Funny old thing, religion.

     PAUSE

2   They got as far as Jacob's well

1   I've heard of that

2   So you should, Jacob's well is famous

1   What for?

2   Jacob sitting, wishing for a drink and a wife

1   Did he get them?

2   Yes, water so clear you could see the bacteria in it

1   And I suppose a woman just happened to come along?

2   Right! Wells are good places for wishing.

PAUSE

1   Well, Jesus rested by this well

2   While his friends went to the Kosher Tesco for a takeaway

1   Jesus wished he had a drink

2   Wished he had a bucket

1   Just like old Jacob, then

2   Only it wasn't really a wishing well.

1   Then this woman came along to get water

2   Where did I hear that before?

1   Only this was different

2   This woman had been around a bit

1   Oh, oh . . .

2   With a bit of a reputation

1   Well!

2   For getting through husbands like an orang-utan through bananas

1   But they'd all died happy

2   Serial monogamy

1   Like . . . bite-sized Wedded Sheet cereal.

2   Did Jesus know about her?

1   Oh yes, he was no fool

2   Just as well.

PAUSE

1   Well, Jesus said:

3   *Give me a drink, love, while you're pouring*

4   *Hang on sunshine, you're not one of us, you're one of them*

3   *We all are, sometimes. And we all need water*

4   *That's true*

3   *I can give you water that's really alive*

4   *What, with tadpoles as well as bacteria?*

3   *Better than that. Pure and life-giving*

4   *Sounds good*

3   *With what I give, you'll never be thirsty again*

4   *I'll take that for my old man – he drinks like he's got blotting paper in his boots*

3   *That's man number 6 in your life, is it?*

4   *Oh yes, you're definitely one of them, if you listen to gossip.*

1   Because she didn't know

2   And we usually forget

1   That God knows everything about everybody

2   And Jesus was like God.

1   Besides which, the well was a holy place

2   Like Jerusalem

1   And funny things happen in holy places

2   Like, for instance?

1   Like, for instance . . .

4   *If you're so clever, tell me where I ought to worship, here or in Jerusalem*

3   *You can meet God anywhere*

4   *Doesn't have to be a mountain*

3   *Nor a Temple*

4   *Nor a synagogue?*

3   *Nor a church.*

4   *I don't think God's in the Kosher Tesco*

3   *God is Spirit, he is everywhere*

4   *Life gets complicated, doesn't it? Roll on the Messiah,*
     then all our religions will get sorted out

3   *You are right. I am he. The water I bring is refreshment for your soul.*

PAUSE

1   So the woman ran off

2   Leaving her bucket

1   Which was handy

2   Feeling a bit peculiar

1   You often do

2   When you meet Jesus

1   Just ask his friends!

2   Who happened to come back just then, bringing the lunch

1   And saw her running away.

2   Hello, hello!

1   They thought

2   What's he been up to now?

1   Because you never can tell

2   What God gets up to

1   And when Jesus meets you

2   And knows how you feel

1   Sometimes you feel all funny inside

2   All weak and watery

1   But strong and bubbly

2   Just like he said about living water inside you.

     PAUSE

1   When the woman got home

2   Without the bucket

1   Without fresh water

2   She said she wasn't going back

1   Without company

2   Well, would you?

1   So some men who had the afternoon free

2   Fancied a bit of messiah-ing

1   Went up the hill

2   Like Jack and Jill

1   To find this living water.

2   What they found was Jesus

1   And his friends

2   And invited them all to come for tea

1   With proper boiling hot water.

2   They got talking

1   As you do

2   About religion and politics

1   And kings and messiahs

2   Until a couple of days went by

1   By which time

2   Jesus had convinced them

1   He was God's Messiah

2   And they all said

1   God save us all!

2   And he does! He does!

Sources

These are the conventional names given to the stories in this collection, with the Gospel references.

1. The sower   *Mark 4:3-9 and parallels*

2. The wicked tenants   *Mark 12:1-9 and parallels*

3. Building a tower   *Luke 14:28-30*

4. The labourers in the vineyard   *Matthew 20:1-16*

5. The wise and foolish virgins   *Matthew 25:1-13*

6. The unjust judge   *Luke 18:1-8*

7. The prodigal son   *Luke 15:11-32*

8. The Pharisee and the publican   *Luke 18:9-14*

9. The hidden treasure and the priceless pearl   *Matthew 13:44-46*

10. The rich fool   *Luke 12:16-21*

11. The wise and foolish builders   *Matthew 7:24-27 and parallels*

12. The rich man (Dives) and Lazarus   *Luke 16:19-31*

13. Jesus and the Samaritan woman   *John 4:4-26*